IN THIS ISSUE:

ISSUE 06 JUNE 2017

PUBLISHER
Tourism Tattler (Pty) Ltd.
PO Box 891, Umhlanga Rocks, 4320
KwaZulu-Natal, South Africa.
Website: www.tourismtattler.com

EXECUTIVE EDITOR Des Langkilde
Cell: +27 (0)82 374 7260
Fax: +27 (0)86 651 8080
E-mail: editor@tourismtattler.com
Skype: tourismtattler

MAGAZINE ADVERTISING
ADVERTISING DIRECTOR Bev Langkilde
Cell: +27 (0)71 224 9971
Fax: +27 (0)86 656 3860
E-mail: bev@tourismtattler.com
Skype: bevtourismtattler

SUBSCRIPTIONS
http://eepurl.com/bocldD

BACK ISSUES (Click on the covers below).

▼ MAY 2017 | ▼ APR 2017 | ▼ MAR 2017

▼ FEB 2017 | ▼ JAN 2017 | ▼ DEC 2016

▼ NOV 2016 | ▼ OCT 2016 | ▼ SEP 2016

▼ AUG 2016 | ▼ JUL 2016 | ▼ JUN 2016

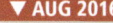

CONTENTS

EDITOR'S DESK
07 The UNWTO Secretary-General Election Fiasco

AFRICA: SUSTAINABLE TOURISM SOLUTIONS
08 Thrivability in Green Hotel Development
10 Join Fair Trade To Move Toward Sustainability
11 Eco & Sustainable Tourism Icons

SOUTH AFRICA: ECO-FRIENDLY HOTELS & LODGES
12 Shamwari Game Reserve
13 Marine Dynamics

SUSTAINABLE TOURISM DESTINATION
14 Supporting Sustainable Tourism Projects in Rwanda

BUSINESS & FINANCE
16 South African Tourism Statistics: Jan-Apr 2017
17 Exclusive Use Safari Lodges on the Rise

CONSERVATION
18 Rehabilitating Benin's Pendjari National Park

DESTINATIONS
21 Exploring Mauritius Resorts
24 Quick Guide to Southern Africa

EVENTS
30 LGBT Pride Month 2017

EDITORIAL CONTRIBUTORS
Adam Jacot de Boinod — José Pliya
Des Langkilde — Martin Janse van Vuuren

MAGAZINE SPONSORS
03 Hotel Verde Azam, Zanzibar — **12** Shamwari Game Reserve
05 The Hotel Show Africa — **13** Marine Dynamics
06 Pan-African Health Tourism Congress — **17** Lalibela Private Game Reserve
08 Verde Hotels — **20** ATA Congress 2017

SUPPORTED CHARITIES
Diabetes South Africa

Disclaimer: The Tourism Tattler is published by Tourism Tattler (Pty) Ltd and is the official trade journal of various trade 'associations' (see page 02). The Tourism Tattler digital e-zine, is distributed free of charge to bona fide tourism stakeholders. Letters to the Editor are assumed intended for publication in whole or part and may therefore be used for such purpose. The information provided and opinions expressed in this publication are provided in good faith and do not necessarily represent the opinions of Tourism Tattler (Pty) Ltd, its 'Associations', its staff and its production suppliers. Advice provided herein should not be soley relied upon as each set of circumstances may differ. Professional advice should be sought in each instance. Neither Tourism Tattler (Pty) Ltd, its 'Associations', its staff and its production suppliers can be held legally liable in any way for damages of any kind whatsoever arising directly or indirectly from any facts or information provided or omitted in these pages or from any statements made or withheld or from supplied photographs or graphic images reproduced by the publication.

Trade Association PARTNER

PROMOTING TOURISM TO
AFRICA
FROM ALL CORNERS OF THE WORLD

Recognised as the Voice of African Tourism, Atta reaches across 22 countries in Africa, showcasing over 530 elite buyers and suppliers of African tourism product.

- Leading role at trade shows around the world
- Networking opportunities
- Industry representation on international commitees & the media
- Interactive platform for information & education
- Daily news service on all aspects of African tourism
- Network of specialist consultants

Join our knowledgeable and experienced membership to increase awareness and visibility of your company

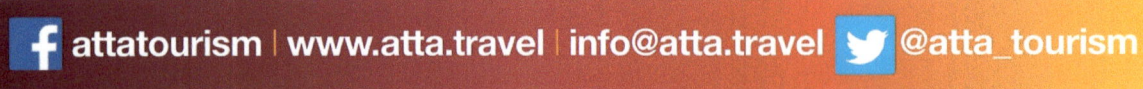

attatourism | www.atta.travel | info@atta.travel | @atta_tourism

Lead Sponsor | Working in partnership with Atta

SOUTH AFRICAN AIRWAYS
A STAR ALLIANCE MEMBER

ZANZIBAR
5* LUXURY FAMILY HEALTH & WELLNESS RESORT

Hotel Verde Azam Luxury Resort will be Zanzibar's greenest 5* luxury hotel. Situated 2km from Stone Town in Mtoni, this world-class redevelopment of the old Mtoni Marine Hotel is set to take sustainable development to new heights in East Africa, becoming a flagship for tourism in Zanzibar and Tanzania.

 5 luxury penthouses

 101 standard rooms

 2 restaurants

 Conferencing facilities (300pax capacity)

 Gala events (250pax capacity)

 Adult & childrens gym, yoga & pilates

 State-of-the-art spa & beauty

 Marina

 Water park

 Water activities

 Childrens entertainment

 Catering & services embracing Islamic principles

OPENING END 2017

info@verdehotels.com | +27 (0) 21 380 5600 | www.verdehotels.com

EDITORIAL

ACCREDITATION

Official Travel Trade Journal and Media Partner to:

The Africa Travel Association (ATA)
Tel: +1 212 447 1357 • Email: info@africatravelassociation.org • Website: www.africatravelassociation.org

ATA is a division of the Corporate Council on Africa (CCA), and a registered non-profit trade association in the USA, with headquarters in Washington, DC and chapters around the world. ATA is dedicated to promoting travel and tourism to Africa and strengthening intra-Africa partnerships. Established in 1975, ATA provides services to both the public and private sectors of the industry.

The African Travel & Tourism Association (Atta)
Tel: +44 20 7937 4408 • Email: info@atta.travel • Website: www.atta.travel

Members in 22 African countries and 37 worldwide use Atta to: Network and collaborate with peers in African tourism; Grow their online presence with a branded profile; Ask and answer specialist questions and give advice; and Attend key industry events.

National Accommodation Association of South Africa (NAA-SA)
Tel: +27 86 186 2272 • Fax: +2786 225 9858 • Website: www.naa-sa.co.za

The NAA-SA is a network of mainly smaller accommodation providers around South Africa – from B&Bs in country towns offering comfortable personal service to luxurious boutique city lodges with those extra special touches – you're sure to find a suitable place, and at the same time feel confident that your stay at an NAA-SA member's establishment will meet your requirements.

Regional Tourism Organisation of Southern Africa (RETOSA)
Tel: +27 11 315 2420/1 • Fax: +27 11 315 2422 • Website: www.retosa.co.za

RETOSA is a Southern African Development Community (SADC) institution responsible for tourism growth and development. RETOSA's aims are to increase tourist arrivals to the region through. RETOSA Member States are Angola, Botswana, DR Congo, Lesotho, Madagascar, Malawi, Mauritius, Mozambique, Namibia, Seychelles, South Africa, Swaziland, Tanzania, Zambia and Zimbabwe.

Southern African Vehicle Rental and Leasing Association (SAVRALA)
Contact: manager@savrala.co.za • Website: www.savrala.co.za

Founded in the 1970's, SAVRALA is the representative voice of Southern Africa's vehicle rental, leasing and fleet management sector. Our members have a combined national footprint with more than 600 branches countrywide. SAVRALA are instrumental in steering industry standards and continuously strive to protect both their members' interests, and those of the public, and are therefore widely respected within corporate and government sectors.

Seychelles Hospitality & Tourism Association (SHTA)
Tel: +248 432 5560 • Fax: +248 422 5718 • Website: www.shta.sc

The Seychelles Hospitality and Tourism Association was created in 2002 when the Seychelles Hotel Association merged with the Seychelles Hotel and Guesthouse Association. SHTA's primary focus is to unite all Seychelles tourism industry stakeholders under one association in order to be better prepared to defend the interest of the industry and its sustainability as the pillar of the country's economy.

International Coalition of Tourism Partners (ICTP)
Website: www.tourismpartners.org
ICTP is a travel and tourism coalition of global destinations committed to Quality Services and Green Growth.

International Institute for Peace through Tourism
Website: www.iipt.org
IIPT is dedicated to fostering tourism initiatives that contribute to international understanding and cooperation.

ITB Asia 2017
Website: www.itb-asia.com
25 to 27 October 2017 Marina Bay Sands®, Singapore.
ITB Asia is the leading B2B travel trade event for the entire Asia-Pacific region.

Tourism, Hotel Investment and Networking Conference 2017
Website: www.thincafrica..com
THINC Africa 2017 takes place in Cape Town, South Africa from 6-7 September.

The Hotel Show Africa 2017
Website: TheHotelShowAfrica.com
Thousands of hospitality professionals from around the world will be at Gallagher Convention Centre in Johannesburg from 25-27 June.

The Safari Awards
Website: www.safariawards.com
Safari Award finalists are amongst the top 3% in Africa and the winners are unquestionably the best.

PAN-AFRICAN HEALTH TOURISM CONGRESS 2017
BUSINESS OPPORTUNITY FAIR & EXHIBITION

PAHTC 2017
Website: www.panafricanhealthtourismcongress.com
08-09 June 2017 at the City of uMhlathuze in KwaZulu-Natal, South Africa.
The Pan-African Health Tourism Congress is being staged to address the interests and needs of Health Tourism Stakeholders in Africa.

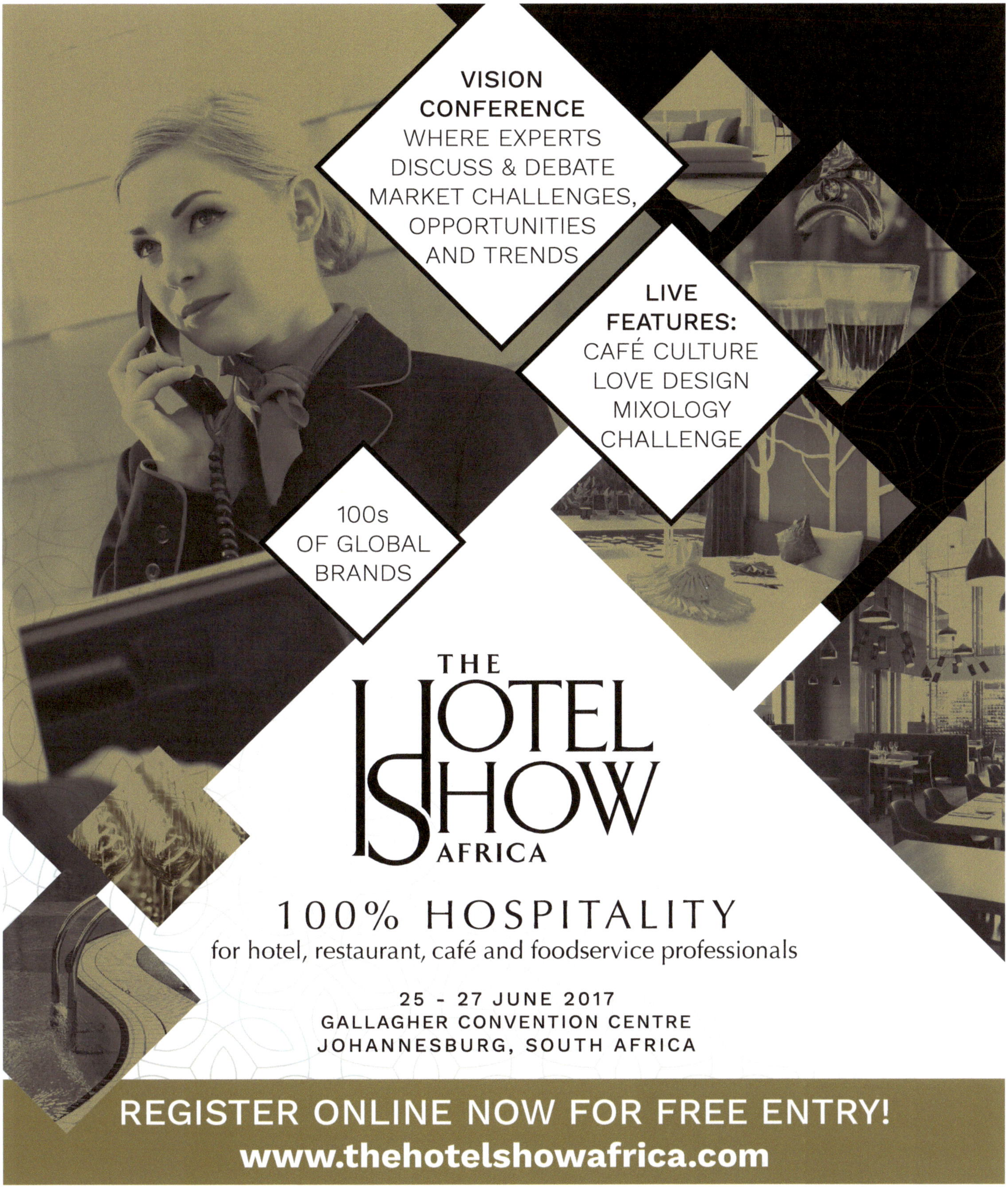

THE Hotel Show AFRICA

VISION CONFERENCE — WHERE EXPERTS DISCUSS & DEBATE MARKET CHALLENGES, OPPORTUNITIES AND TRENDS

LIVE FEATURES: CAFÉ CULTURE · LOVE DESIGN · MIXOLOGY CHALLENGE

100s OF GLOBAL BRANDS

100% HOSPITALITY
for hotel, restaurant, café and foodservice professionals

25 - 27 JUNE 2017
GALLAGHER CONVENTION CENTRE
JOHANNESBURG, SOUTH AFRICA

REGISTER ONLINE NOW FOR FREE ENTRY!
www.thehotelshowafrica.com

BUSINESS EVENT MEDIA PARTNER

Co-located with:

Strategic Partners:

Powered by: HOTEL & RESTAURANT

Organised by:  dmg::ems africa

AWAKENING AFRICA'S HEALTH TOURISM INDUSTRY

The City of uMhlathuze, Proud host of
THE PAN-AFRICAN HEALTH TOURISM CONGRESS

BUSINESS OPPORTUNITY FAIR & EXHIBITION

08-09 June 2017

Umfolozi Hotel Casino Convention Resort
Empangeni, uMhlathuze
KwaZulu-Natal, South Africa

Book your seat!
Tel. +27 11 040 7351-4
registrar@mcgroup.co.za
www.panafricanhealthtourismcongress.com

FROM THE EDITOR'S DESK

UNWTO Secretary-General Election FIASCO

When I wrote '**The Race for UNWTO Secretary-General**' on 11 April, I had high hopes on the Seychelles candidate Alain St.Ange winning the race. At the time, I could not have foreseen that this esteemed institution would become embroiled in scandal and political intrigue, and subsequently dash Africa's chance of taking the helm to steer the UNWTO into the global future of tourism.

By **Des Langkilde**.

To appreciate the intrigue, let's recount the course of events as they unfolded before and after the fateful day of the election when Georgian candidate Zurab Pololikashvili was nominated UNWTO Secretary-General for the 2018-2022 period.

On 20 April, Ethiopia submitted an urgent letter to the ministers in charge of tourism in Congo, Uganda, Ethiopia, Cameroon, Sierra Leone, Zambia, Ghana, Morocco, Nigeria, Zimbabwe, Niger, Kenya, Gambia, Benin, Burkina Faso, Sudan, Angola, and the Democratic Republic of Congo, urging them to support a letter to be submitted to the Chairperson of the African Union Commission urging him to approach the Republic of the Seychelles *"to put the interest of Africa first and to withdraw their candidature* (of Alain St.Ange) *and work with* (Zimbabwe's candidate) *Walter Mzembi in order for Africa to enhance its chances of winning this position."*

Considering that Seychelles is an active member of both the Southern African Development Community (SADC) and the African Union (AU), the island state would have been involved in the decision to "unanimously" endorse Mzembi as Africa's candidate at respective meetings convened in March 2016 in Gaborone, Botswana, and in July 2016 in Kigali, Rwanda.

Why then did the Seychelles President Danie Faure subsequently accept St.Ange's conscientious letter of resignation from his position as Minister of Tourism, Civil Aviation, Ports & Marine on 29 December 2016? In fact, the Seychelles News Agency actually issued a statement from the president's office on Wednesday 28th stating that Minister St.Ange intends to apply for the post of Secretary-General of the World Tourism Organisation. By doing so, the president effectively endorsed St.Ange's candidacy, a fact that was confirmed when St.Ange presented his official documents (which had to include a letter of endorsement from his country) to formalise his candidature during the FITUR tourism trade fair in Madrid, Spain in January 2017.

The AU finally got around to submitting the aforementioned letter to the Seychelles via its member representative Zambia, demanding that the island state immediately withdraws its candidate from the race, effectively blackmailing the Seychelles with implied threats of economic sanctions by AU member states.

On 9 May, just two days before the UNWTO elections were to take place in Spain, President Faure chaired an Extra-Ordinary Cabinet meeting at which the Seychelles Cabinet agreed to withdraw the candidature of St.Ange for the position of Secretary General. *"Seychelles will stand in solidarity with the African Union and support the African Union's officially endorsed candidate from Zimbabwe in the upcoming election."* read the official announcement.

Of course, St.Ange was already in Madrid at the time (at his own expense I must add) to lobby for his countries candidature when the news broke.

One can only imagine his surprise and extreme disappointment when he heard of his countries back peddling. Months of travelling the globe, sleepless nights, lobbying for support, and significant personal expenditure had just gone down the drain, not to mention his embarrassment at having to disappoint countless supporters, many of whom had officially submitted letters of endorsement to the UNWTO.

Following the 11 May elections, it has become apparent that controversy surrounds the nomination of Albania's Zurab Polokashvili. Unlike other candidates, Pololikashvili barely attended any UNWTO events before or after his election, but he did attend and invite selected delegates to a football game in Madrid on 10 May. The accusation is that Pololikashvili handpicked voting executive members of the UNWTO to oblige and impress them by sponsoring football tickets that were almost impossible to get – all during the ongoing Executive Council conference.

Further allegations of fraud, payoffs, and unethical (if not illegal) manipulation outside of the world of tourism surrounds Pololikashvili and may cost Georgia the reconfirmation of their candidate's nomination when the UNWTO General Assembly convenes in China on 11 September 2017.

The world of tourism is crying "foul" as attested to by comments received to an opinion poll conducted by eTN's UNWTOWire website.

Pololikashvili's nomination needs 2/3 of all member countries attending the September General Assembly to agree before Georgia is ratified to lead the UN Agency as of 2018.

According to eTN, confirming a nominee at past elections was no big deal, except for a near-tied score for a third term of France's Francesco Francalli at the UNWTO General Assembly in Senegal, after Spain raised objections.

So what happens if Georgia's nomination is rejected? There is no clear rule in place. According to verbal statements related to eTN as coming from the current secretary-general Taleb Rifai, the General Assembly may refer the election back to the new Executive Council, which will be comprised of different member states and could meet early in 2018. Alternately, Rifai could stay on or appoint a deputy to lead affairs after his term ends in December 2017.

Should any of the above scenarios transpire, I doubt that the SADC and AU would change their stance in supporting Zimbabwe. I also doubt that Seychelles would stand up to threats of AU sanctions even if St.Ange is willing to stand as the island's candidate for another round.

SUSTAINABLE TOURISM SOLUTIONS

Thrivability in Green Hotel Development

The lessons learned in sustainable development and marketing of 'Africa's Greenest Hotel' in Cape Town and 'Zanzibar's Greenest Resort' in Tanzania is now being offered as a turnkey solution for hospitality investors worldwide through Verde Hotels.

By **Des Langkilde**.

Hotelier Mario Delicio and his industrious team at Verde Hotels have an ambitious aim – to establish green hotels throughout Africa, and abroad.

"I had never imagined that my families' humble pursuit to own a green hotel would become the exceptionally caring and inventive establishment that Hotel Verde Cape Town has become. I hope that people will see all of our cumulative efforts and that they will be inspired to implement small changes in their lives and businesses too," says Mario.

And the "small changes" that Mario eludes to are coined in the phrase 'Thrivability' – meaning the act of thriving and prospering without damaging or causing harm and encompassing three core concepts: People, Profit, and Planet.

"Our approach to sustainable tourism development is about neutralising a hotel's impact on the environment and about succeeding as a business venture. Thrivability speaks to the business imperative of making a profit

Energy. In addition to energy produced by the indoor gym, Hotel Verde also has photo-voltaic solar panels and three wind turbines, producing 11,9% of their energy requirement per annum.

Outdoor Gym. Verde Hotels' flagship hotel at Cape Town International Airport, Hotel Verde, uses a dedicated outdoor gym area to assist guests to engage with the environment.

in order to perpetuate an organization (and its members/employees) as well as function in productive symbiosis with its environment," says Samantha Annandale, CEO of Verde Hotels.

Verde Hotel's thrivability model provides sustainable hospitality solutions that meet stringent international green building certification system criteria. The model incorporates responsible design, construction, project, and operations management and training. As pioneers in green hospitality globally, Verde Hotels provides socially conscious investors, developers, and hoteliers with significantly reduced operating costs and increased profits by providing turnkey service offerings focused on new commercial construction and retrofitting of existing buildings.

"When we built Hotel Verde in 2012 we paid a premium of nearly 11% to build green. At that time we were expecting an ROI of around 7 years. However, the power crisis two years ago, and the water crisis now, have seen energy costs rise tremendously and due to this, our ROI has reduced down to 5 years. Today, so many products are available at no extra cost and other products such as solar PV panels have come down in cost to the point that the premium of going green today is only 7-8%. I'm not exaggerating when I say that green building is the only viable way considering that the savings over time are so great," says Delicio.

Isolating quantifiable ROI's, the green build project gained just over R30 million in free press exposure since the project commenced, reduced utility consumption costs by 70% (cost per room night based on utilities at Hotel Verde was R29.52 vs an average Cape Town hotel of R97.28 cost), and lowered energy consumption by 63,1% (94 kWh/sqm/annum vs Cape Town hotel average of 255 kWh/sqm/annum), which even beat the LEED model average of 159.5 kWh/sqm/annum by 41,4%.

Overall, the Hotel Verde green-build project resulted in an average of 35% lower operating costs, a 70% reduction in energy consumption, 92% waste to landfill reduction, and 64.9% lower water consumption.

"At Verde Hotels we believe that the hotel industry has changed, and hoteliers simply cannot build or operate hotels in the same way as they have done in the past. Verde Hotels is the future of hospitality. Companies with proactive environmental strategies have a 4% higher return on investment, 9% higher sales growth and 17% higher operating growth than companies with poor environmental track records," says Samantha.

As a hotel management company, Verde Hotels aims to spearhead sustainable hotel management throughout Africa by offering hotel investors and developers property management packages for both new construction projects and retrofitting of existing buildings.

For more information visit www.verdehotels.co.za or contact Samantha at info@verdehotels.co.za or call +27 21 380 5600.

Download the **Verde Hotels Corporate Overview** HERE

Water. A 40 000 Litre water tank collects rain water for landscape irrigation, while a Pontos grey water plant sterilises and filters guest shower and basin water, which is pumped back into the Hotel to flush the toilet system.

Join Fair Trade To Move Toward Sustainability

Fair Trade Tourism (FTT) launched a new membership programme in May aimed at tourism businesses that need support for their sustainability measures but do not have the resources to become certified in the short term.

For an annual membership fee, ranging from 1,100 (ZAR) for a sole enterprise to 6,000 (ZAR) for a business with 26-50 staff members, Fair Trade Tourism will guide businesses along the sustainability path, focusing on areas such as legal compliance, labour and staff management, reducing energy, water and waste, fair purchasing and improving market access.

Commenting on the entry level programme, Jane Edge, Managing Director of FTT said: "Our aim is to bring smaller businesses into the Fair Trade Tourism value chain, to encourage them to operate more sustainably and to expose them to tour operators who support sustainable efforts. By lowering the threshold for enterprises to access our business development services, we hope to broaden our sustainability impact and contribute to more inclusive growth of the tourism industry."

Aspirant members need to be approved by FTT's Client Advisory Committee and to sign a pledge committing them to year-on-year improvements in their sustainability measures. Applicants fill out a self-evaluation form online about their sustainability actions and FTT will produce a gap analysis highlighting areas where the business needs to improve. FTT will provide the toolkits, templates, and advice required to assist businesses along the sustainability path.

For more information, contact Thiofhi Ravele, Business Development Services Manager at *thiofhi@fairtrade.travel* or apply online on at *www.fairtrade.travel*.

Fair Trade Tourism has partnered with Tourism Tattler in supporting the aims and aspirations of the
2017 International Year of Sustainable Tourism for Development.
Through a series of editorial features published throughout this year, Tourism Tattler will be profiling a selection of Fair Trade certified tourism businesses who meet and in many cases exceed, sustainable tourism practices.

View Fair Trade's Sustainable Tourism Gems already listed on the
UNWTO #IYSTD2017 official website at:
www.tourism4development2017.org

PARTNER — SPECIAL FEATURE — AFRICA'S SUSTAINABLE TOURISM GEMS

HOME SEARCH ○ ABOUT ○ GET INVOLVED ○ BLOG ○ CONTACT US | GET LISTED ON ECO ATLAS ✓

Launching Africa's sustainable tourism gems this month with a selection of South Africa's eco-friendly hotels and lodges, Tourism Tattler has partnered with Eco Atlas – an award winning eco-travel choice website. Where a featured eco-friendly property is already listed on Eco Atlas, we've shown the applicable icons.

RESOURCE USE

 **Water Saving:** 3 or more of the following practices in place: a no-leak policy, water audit, flow restrictors on taps and shower heads, dual flush toilet cisterns, harvesting rain water, utilising waste water (grey water), only watering early morning and evening, alien tree removal, planting water wise, drip irrigation system, compost toilet, garden well mulched.

 **Energy Saving:** 3 or more of the following practices in place: energy A- rated appliances, low energy bulbs, geezer blankets and/or timers, established electricity strategy such as switching off appliances and lights when not being used.

 **Recycling:** Established policy to reduce and re-use waste, the recycling of any of the following resources: Paper, Glass, Tin, Plastic and Organic Matter, on-site composting and wormeries.

 **Renewable Energy:** Utilising solar and/or wind energy through solar panels and/or wind turbines.

 **Green Design:** Incorporated into the design of the building: proper insulation, sustainable and renewable building materials, maximising light and energy from the sun, building with recycled materials, non-toxic paints and other building materials, water and energy efficiency.

 **Carbon Neutral:** Planting of trees to off-set the carbon footprint of the establishment and its guests.

EARTH FRIENDLY

 **Eco Cleaning Agents:** utilising or selling products that are fully biodegradable, free of harmful chemicals and not tested on animals.

 **Eco Body Products:** Utilising or selling body products that are fully biodegradable, free of harmful chemicals and not tested on animals.

 **Eco Packaging:** Utilising or selling fully biodegradable packaging and take-away containers made from renewable resources. Accepting returns on product packaging for re-use.

PEOPLE AND EARTH

 **Biodiversity:** no use of pesticides or poisons, planting only indigenous, conservation of indigenous flora and fauna on your property, alien vegetation removal and rehabilitation of indigenous.

 **Local Products:** utilising products grown or manufactured within a 100km radius, the producing or selling of local products.

 **Organic Food:** Utilising or selling food that is produced using a system that sustains the health of soils, ecosystems and people without the use of inputs with adverse effects for biodiversity.

 **Fair Trade:** selling products or implementing policies which contribute to sustainable development by offering better trading conditions to, and securing the rights of, marginalized producers and workers. Registered with Fair Trade Tourism or Fair Trade Label SA.

 **Empowerment:** Skills development, training and profit share programmes which empower staff and enable better working conditions and work opportunities.

ANIMAL FRIENDLY

 **Free Range Chicken:** raised in a humane manner with freedom to roam and constant access to vegetation, fresh air and fresh water. Chickens free of hormones and antibiotics (check with your supplier if they meet all these requirements)

 **Free Range Eggs:** chickens raised in a humane manner with freedom to roam and constant access to vegetation, fresh air and fresh water. Chickens free of hormones and antibiotics (check with your supplier if they meet all these requirements)

 **Badger Friendly Honey:** utilising or selling honey accredited with the Endangered Wildlife Trust certificate to ensure no honey badgers are harmed in the production of the honey.

 **Ethically Farmed Products:** utilising or selling free range meat and/or wool products that are have wildlife friendly management strategies which do not include the trapping, hunting, poisoning and killing of predators. Fair Game endorsed products.

 **Sustainable Fishing:** utilising, promoting or selling sustainable seafood from well managed fisheries as listed in the South African Sustainable Seafood Initiative (SASSI).

 **Free Range Pork:** Raised in a humane manner with freedom to roam outdoors and constant access to vegetation, fresh air and fresh water. Pigs free of hormones and antibiotics and their feed free of animal by-products (check with your supplier if they meet all these requirements)

 **Veg Or Vegan:** Serving purely vegetarian or vegan food, thereby providing healthy eating alternatives and decreasing the amount of natural resources used in the production of food.

AFRICA'S SUSTAINABLE TOURISM GEMS — SPECIAL FEATURE — SOUTH AFRICA

ECO-FRIENDLY HOTELS & LODGES & ATTRACTIONS

Marine Dynamics

Taking eco-tourists on captivating trips at sea to cage dive with Great White Sharks and meet the rest of the Marine Big 5 is only a glimpse of many things that Marine Dynamics do to protect and conserve the critically important Dyer Island ecosystem around Gansbaai in the Western Cape.

Marine Dynamics Shark Tours and Dyer Island Cruises whale watching have been Fair Trade Tourism certified since 2008 and in 2016 added their successful International Marine Volunteer Programme.

Marine Dynamics' Responsible Tourism Policy is a credo that the group businesses all adhere to: "Our every activity is driven by our motto *'Discover and Protect'*. We consciously and actively: operate responsibly with due care for the marine and terrestrial environment; conduct ethical scientific research, which contributes to the conservation of species; create conservation awareness amongst locals and visitors; contribute positively to the community and the economy in which we operate; offer fair wages and good working conditions for our employees; and contribute positively to the protection of cultural heritage."

Marine Dynamics is the eco-tourism partner of the owner established Dyer Island Conservation Trust helping save the endangered African penguin, the vulnerable great white shark through effective research, supporting community education, marine animal rescues, and marine pollution efforts. Visit their key project, the African Penguin and Seabird Sanctuary on your next trip to Gansbaai. **YOUR CHOICE MAKES A DIFFERENCE.**

Travel. Enjoy. Respect. #IYSTD2017

QUICK LINKS:

- +27 (082 280 3405 / +27 (0)28 384 1005
- www.sharkwatchsa.com
- dive@sharkwatchsa.com
- @MarineDynamics
- @MarineDynamics
- www.sharkwatchsa.com/en/blog
- Marine Dynamics Shark Tours

Marine Dynamics

SOUTH AFRICA | SPECIAL FEATURE | AFRICA'S SUSTAINABLE TOURISM GEMS

Shamwari Game Reserve

Shamwari Game Reserve, the pride of the Eastern Cape, is one of the largest malaria-free Big-5 private game reserves in the region, offering 6 distinctive lodges and the seasonal Explorer Camp – a two-day walking safari in tented accommodation. With pioneering safaris, conservation, and 5-star hospitality, Shamwari welcomes guests looking for genuine conservation experiences. Shamwari is a proud member of Fair Trade Tourism and 2017 marks Shamwari's 25th anniversary.

Guests can learn about conservation at the Animal Rehabilitation Centre, the Born Free Foundation or the Ian Player Rhino Awareness Centre whilst budding photographers can take advantage of the Pro Photo Safari to perfect their skills.

In addition to being passionate about nature conservation, Shamwari believes in educating and inspiring children, so younger guests can enjoy the Kids on Safari programme. The Relaxation Retreats offer treatments and therapies to awaken the senses and allow guests to rejuvenate body, mind, and soul.

So whether it is the call of the African bush to embrace the phenomenal flora and fauna that only Africa offers or you're in search of a family or romantic honeymoon retreat, Shamwari is waiting for you to help conserve a vanishing way of life!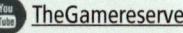

Read Tattler's Property Review: Long Lee Manor at Shamwari.

QUICK LINKS:

📞 +27 (0)42 203 1111 ✉ reservations@shamwari.com
🏠 www.shamwari.com 📝 shamwari.com/blog f @shamwarisafari
🐦 @ShamwariSafari 📷 shamwari_game_reserve ▶ TheGamereserve

#MarineBig5
Year Round Tours

SHARK ALLEY
34° 41, 246' S
19° 24, 790 E

Supporting Sustainable Tourism in Rwanda

By **Des Langkilde**.

Rwanda should be congratulated for increasing the price of its gorilla permits. Considering what the funds are used for, it's a small price to pay in support of the country's sustainable tourism projects.

Rwanda is well-known for its mountain gorillas, with gorilla trekking being its main tourist attraction. This endangered species has made a significant contribution to the nation's travel and tourism industry thanks to events such as the Kwita Izina gorilla naming ceremony and the conservation efforts of the Rwandan government, which seeks to ensure the safety and long-term sustainability of its gorilla population in order to maintain the constant flow of tourists to the country.

Overtourism - a phrase that refers to the negative impact that hosting too many tourists simultaneously can have on a destination's natural assets - is a valid concern. Perhaps then it is understandable that as custodians, the Rwanda Development Board announced on 6 May 2017 that the price of gorilla permits will increase from US$ 750 to US $1,500 for all visitors with immediate effect. The price increase will not affect tourists who had already purchased their tickets prior to, or at the time of this announcement.

Tourists who visit other national parks (Nyungwe and Akagera) for a minimum of three days, in addition to gorilla trekking will receive a discount of 30%. Similarly, conference tourists, who stay pre or post conference dates to see gorillas will be eligible for a 15% discount.

In line with Rwanda's high-end tourism strategy, the price increase aims to strengthen conservation efforts and contribute more to the development of communities living around the Volcanoes National Park.

Along with the new tariff, the tourism revenue sharing rate for communities adjacent to the park, will also increase from 5% to 10%, which will quadruple the absolute revenues received by communities.

Over the last 12 years, more than 400 community projects have been completed including hospitals, schools, business development centers and water supply systems to facilitate access to clean water. These projects directly benefit the people living around the parks.

Commenting on the gorilla permit price increases, Ms. Clare Akamanzi, the Chief Executive Officer at Rwanda Development Board said: "Gorilla trekking is a highly unique experience. We have raised the price of permits in order to ensure sustainability of conservation initiatives and enhance visitors' experience. We also want to make sure that the communities living near the park area receive a bigger share of tourism revenues to fund development projects and empower them economically."

New, high-end lodges are opening in Musanze and plans are underway to improve visitors' experience at Kinigi, including renovation of the information center to equip it with modern offices and tourism services such as conservation education, children's learning space as well as digital facilities.

In terms of tourism attractions, Rwanda is not just about tracking for gorillas, which too many visitors fly in to see then leave, missing out on this countries many treasures, such as:

Primates. Rwanda is home to one fifth of the primate species in Africa. These include the golden monkeys, chimpanzees, black and white colobus monkeys and many more.

Avitourim: Rwanda boasts one of the highest concentrations of birds in Africa, with over 700 species of bird, 27 of which are endemic to the Albertine rift.

Mountain gorillas are an endangered species with only around 880 remaining in the world. Of those in in the Virunga Massif, Rwanda accounts for 62% of the gorilla population. Stringent conservation measures have significantly contributed to a rise in gorilla numbers. There are currently 20 families habituated for tourism and research in Rwanda, up from just 9 families in 2010.

Forests: Nyungwe is one of Africa's oldest mountain rainforests staying green even through the ice age which explains its biodiversity. Home to east Africa's only canopy walkway (70m high and 200m long) it provides an exhilarating chimp's eye view of the forest.

Volcanoes: Hiking to the craters atop the countries stunning mountain volcanoes is exhilarating; the highest point is 4,507m on Karisimbi. The views are just as stunning from the base of these majesticvolcanoes at the park office of Kinigi.

Safari Tourism. Akagera National Park, just two hours from Kigali is home to big game such as elephant,buffalo, leopard, hippo, zebra and giraffe. Lions and Black Rhino have been reintroduced.

Agritourism: Tea is Rwanda's largest export product and these stunning rich green plantations can be seen throughout the country. These 'tours for the senses' take you to tea and coffee plantations and factories where you can sleep, pick, process and taste you morning cuppa.

Historical Tourism: The genocide museum in Kigali gives a look into Rwanda's painful past which has labelled the country for years. The incredibly positive outlook and warm hospitality of this young nation is an impressive turnaround one which has turned them into an inspiration among other African nations.

Beach Tourism: Just one hour drive from the Gorillas are tropical beaches on the shores of lake Kivu where you can relax and unwind or enjoy water sports or boat rides on the lake.

Cultural Tourism: Traditional Intore dancers are a true spectacle to see as they perform their warlike dances with spears and shield. Once only performed for the royal court, this energetic dance can be seen at museums and events throughout the country.

City Tourism. Kigali, the capital city of Rwanda is one of the cleanest most modern cities in Africa with lots of new developments and smart buildings. Roads and pavements are spotless and plastic bags are banned. It is mandatory that everyone participates in acommunity clean up day (Umuganda) on the last Saturday of every month.

Business Tourism. Did you know that the Kigali Convention Centre can seat 2600 delegates, is just 10 minutes from the Kigali International Airport and has 1000 high-end rooms in close proximity? Rwanda is increasingly becoming a destination of choice for international conferences and event organisers.

Rwanda is also the first country in East, Central and North Africa to become a member of the highly prestigious International Council of Tourism Partners (ICTP) – a global alliance of responsible destination cooperation and marketing in tourism. It promotes best practices and being on its list is considered a sign of excellence.

Conclusion

Tourism is a key pillar in the country's Vision 2020 as the top foreign exchange earner and the country's largest employer, but Rwanda still needs revenue from permits and levys to implement its sustainable tourism projects – and that's where your help is invaluable.

For more information visit www.rwandatourism.com and www.rdb.rw

BUSINESS & FINANCE

Market Intelligence Report

SATSA – Southern Africa Tourism Services Association / Grant Thornton

The information below was extracted from data available as at **05 June 2017**. By Martin Jansen van Vuuren of Grant Thornton.

ARRIVALS

The latest available data from Statistics South Africa is for **January to February 2017***:

	Current period	Change over same period last year
UK	102 155	3.7%
Germany	73 497	13.6%
USA	46 770	5.9%
India	12 328	-8.1%
China (incl Hong Kong)	21 137	-3.1%
Overseas Arrivals	500 975	11.4%
African Arrivals	1 308 757	-3.8%
Total Foreign Arrivals	1 816 358	0.0%

HOTEL STATS

The latest available data from STR Global is for **January** to **April 2017**:

Current period	Average Room Occupancy (ARO)	Average Room Rate (ARR)	Revenue Per Available Room (RevPAR)
All Hotels in SA	64.7%	R 1 304	R 844
All 5-star hotels in SA	68.3%	R 2 452	R 1 673
All 4-star hotels in SA	66.4%	R 1 203	R 798
All 3-star hotels in SA	63.4%	R 951	R 603
Change over same period last year			
All Hotels in SA	-1.2%	6.6%	5.3%
All 5-star hotels in SA	-1.1%	6.7%	5.5%
All 4-star hotels in SA	0.4%	6.9%	7.3%
All 3-star hotels in SA	-0.1%	3.7%	3.7%

ACSA DATA

The latest available data from ACSA is for **January** to **April 2017**:

Change over same period last year	Passengers arriving on International Flights	Passengers arriving on Regional Flights	Passengers arriving on Domestic Flights
OR Tambo International	3.3%	-2.6%	0.3%
Cape Town International	27.0%	2.8%	1.3%
King Shaka International	13.6%	N/A	4.5%

CAR RENTAL DATA

The latest available data from SAVRALA is for **January to December 2016**:

	Current period	Change over same period last year
Industry Rental Days	16 936 276	7%
Industry Utilisation	71.6%	1.5%
Industry Revenue	5 294 680 207	12%

WHAT THIS MEANS FOR MY BUSINESS

Even though overseas arrivals are still growing, arrivals from India and China have declined. Occupancy rates have also declined slightly with room rates growing at rates slightly above inflation. It is expected that 2017 will see subdued growth in international arrivals and tourism enterprises are cautioned to reduce costs and increase marketing efforts.

*Note that African Arrivals plus Overseas Arrivals do not add to Total Foreign Arrivals due to the exclusion of unspecified arrivals, which could not be allocated to either African or Overseas.

For more information contact Martin at Grant Thornton on +27 (0)21 417 8338 or visit: http://www.gt.co.za

BUSINESS & FINANCE

Exclusive Use
Safari Lodges
on the Rise

With global demand for exclusive use vacation rentals on the rise, Lalibela Game Reserve is seizing the opportunity by providing a solution for large family and corporate sole-use enquiries who want a Big-5 safari experience with exclusivity and privacy.

By **Des Langkilde**.

"There's no better way to experience a safari when travelling as a group of friends, family or corporate team of colleagues than having your own private villa – your own dedicated chef and personal butler, your own safari vehicle with your own dedicated ranger: this is the ultimate safari experience tailormade to the specific wishes of the vacation rentals market," says Vernon Wait, Marketing Director at Lalibela Private Game Reserve in the malaria-free province of South Africa's Eastern Cape province.

And it seems that Wait is onto something big here. According to LeisureLink, the $100 billion vacation rental sector could be going into over-drive as it attracts growing interest from investors, major hospitality brands and travelers seeking alternate accommodation.

Since the sale of Lalibela to new owners in July 2016, the roll out of numerous projects that include game repopulation, environment rehabilitation, and WiFi service upgrades, has seen occupancy at the game reserve's three lodges increase significantly.

"Thanks to strong relationships with tour operators and travel agents in the distribution chain, we have enjoyed an absolutely bumper 2016 and the first quarter of 2017. But we cannot rest on our laurels. We've received numerous enquiries to cater for large families, and while we have been able to accommodate them at our child-friendly Mark's Camp lodge, we feel that the time is right to offer an exclusive use villa-style option in our portfolio," says Wait.

With this in mind, the historic 100-year old farmhouse, ideally positioned on an elevated site with sweeping views of game browsing on grasslands over the expansive valley below and its own water hole, is in the process of being renovated.

Aptly named **Hillside Private Villa**, this exclusive use home-style villa offering is due to launch in September 2017. Reminiscent of South Africa's bygone colonial era, a time when high wool prices and the ostrich feather boom allowed farmers to build stately family homes, the Edwardian period architectural features are a delight to behold; stately gables, large rooms with high ceilings and wide wrap-around verandas reflect the Eastern Cape's proud heritage.

Facilities inside the Hillside Private Villa include a welcoming bar, spacious lounge and gracious dining room. Outside there is a swimming pool and sun deck, and a large fire pit and barbeque area where al fresco dinners can be served under the African sky. The wide, shady veranda offers cool respite from the sun and a place to relax between game drives.

With 5 double or twin bedrooms, the villa can accommodate a maximum of 10 guests. Three of the rooms have en-suite bathrooms with bath, shower and his and her basins. These rooms have wide stack doors opening out onto the veranda and the indigenous gardens and valley view beyond. The other two bedrooms have en-suite bathrooms with shower and his & her basins. All bedrooms are air-conditioned.

As Lalibela is a Big-5 game reserve, where all game species roam freely, Hillside Private Villa will be discreetly fenced to ensure the safety of guests with small children. Experienced childminders and nannies are available to take care of children while the adults enjoy each other's company in the peace and serenity of Africa's veld interspersed with the occasional plaintive cry of a majestic fish eagle or the rasping call of a Knysna Turaco.

For more information visit www.lalibela.net

CONSERVATION

Rehabilitating Pendjari National Park in Benin

The Presidency of the Republic of Benin and the conservation NGO African Parks announce the signing of a 10-year renewable partnership to revitalise, rehabilitate and develop Pendjari National Park, one of the largest remaining protected reserves in West and Central Africa.

By **José Pliya**.

The total investment of USD$26 million over 10 years will be used to protect and develop the Park spanning 4,800 km2. The revitalisation of Pendjari National Park is one of the 45 flagship projects of the "Revealing Benin" investment programme, announced by the Presidency of the Republic of Benin in December 2016, and is the eleventh park under management by African Parks on the continent.

Pendjari National Park: revitalising an exceptional wildlife reserve

Pendjari National Park, located in the north-west of Benin, is part of the WAP complex (W-Arly-Pendjari) spanning Benin, Burkina Faso and Niger. It is the largest remaining intact ecosystem in the whole of West Africa and the last vast refuge for West African wildlife. With an area of 4,800km2, Pendjari is home to elephant, buffalo, lion, cheetah, antelope and many other species (hippo, tsessebe, Buffon's kob and Defassa waterbuck to name a few).

However, this exceptional reserve faces major threats including poaching, demographic pressure on surrounding land, as well as exponential resource erosion. As a result, the Presidency of the Republic of Benin has quickly put in place a plan to revitalise and protect the Park, as part of its investment programme "Revealing Benin ". In a progressive step the Government of Benin is committing $5.9M over 10 years, and initial start-up funds are being provided by several donors including the Wyss Foundation who made a significant multi-year challenge grant to African Parks to bring new parks under management.

A long-term partnership

By signing a partnership agreement, the Presidency of Benin and African Parks set a goal of doubling the Park's wildlife populations within the next 10 years. The action plan for the Park aims to develop responsible tourism, and to ensure the economic and social development of the region. Three main work streams have been identified:

1. **Security for the inhabitants and the protection of animal species.** Securing Pendjari is the main priority of the agreement. A special brigade will be set up, with the recruitment of 10 officers, non-commissioned officers and specialised technicians, along with the training of 90 guards. A communications and geolocation network will cover the entire site, and all information will be centralised 24 hours a day at the operations coordination centre. A 190 km perimeter fence, 150 km of roads, an operational base, staff quarters, three guard posts and three small airfields will also be constructed.

2. **Conservation of biodiversity.** In order to ensure the success of this partnership, an inventory of all animal species will be carried out every two years. A telemetric or specific monitoring system of key species such as elephants, lions, leopards and cheetahs - the prize species of Pendjari - will be implemented. Scientific research will also be fostered through close collaboration with Beninese and foreign universities and research organisations.

3. **Sustainable economic impact and local community development.** A unique tourist offering will be developed, with the objective of increasing visitors from 6,000 to more than 9,000. The challenge is to generate more direct revenue for the management of the Park, and to do so, African Parks will redevelop and manage the hotel and lodge in Pendjari.

Due to growing demographic pressure (the human population surrounding Pendjari is expected to increase from 50,000 in 2017 to

CONSERVATION

FAST FACTS

Benin, a French-speaking West African nation, is a birthplace of the vodun (or "voodoo") religion and home to the former Dahomey Kingdom from circa 1600–1900. In Abomey, Dahomey's former capital, the Historical Museum occupies two royal palaces with bas-reliefs recounting the kingdom's past and a throne mounted on human skulls. Pendjari National Park lies to the north of Benin.

Capital: Porto-Novo

Dialing code: +229

President: Patrice Talon

Currency: West African CFA franc

Population: 10.88 million (2015) World Bank

Source: Wikipedia

more than 65,000 in the coming 10 years), the integration of local communities in the project is crucial for the long-term conservation of the Park.

Almost 400 direct jobs will be created, with training given to the guards and to professionals of the tourist industry, including guides, reception staff and drivers. Outcomes are also expected to be positive for local crafts, local businesses and markets.

"The Pendjari National Park is an exceptional reserve, which requires us to act quickly to protect and revitalise. Through this partnership, we intend to reveal its full potential. We will put in place the necessary structures to preserve the fauna and the flora, but also make its development sustainable. It is a project of conservation, sustainable tourism and social development." José Pliya, Director of the National Agency for the Heritage and Tourism of Benin, in charge of the implementation of the project for the Presidency of the Republic.

"Pendjari along with the WAP complex is arguably the most important wildlife area and largest intact and functioning ecosystem left in all of West Africa. It's a critical and progressive moment for conservation and the entire region; and we are honoured to enter into this partnership with the Government of Benin, to manage this extraordinary landscape for the benefit of both wildlife and the people of Benin." Peter Fearnhead, CEO of African Parks

The potential for a major tourist destination

The revitalisation of Pendjari National Park is one of the 45 flagship projects of the investment programme "Revealing Benin" launched in December 2016 by the Presidency of Benin. Tourism is one of the strategic sectors targeted by this programme, the objective being to take advantage of the historical, cultural and natural heritage of Benin to develop a tourist industry that provides strong economic outcomes and jobs. Beyond the exceptional fauna and flora, the Afro-Portuguese architecture of Porto-Novo, or the memorials of the slavery trade in Ouidah, are prime examples. The preserved coastline of the country is also a solid asset for the development of a qualitative ecotourism offer.

ABOUT THE REVEALING BENIN PROGRAMME

In December 2016, the Government of the Republic of Benin launched "Revealing Benin", a development and investment programme of unprecedented scale in the country's history. With a budget of 9.039 trillion FCFA (€13.78 billion) over the next five years, it will raise investment to 34% of GDP (compared to 18.8% currently) through a collaboration with private sector partners, who will provide 61% of the programme's total planned investment. Based on 45 major projects across nine key sectors, the programme will sustainably revitalise the country's economy. Discover more on RevealingBenin.com.

ABOUT AFRICAN PARKS

African Parks is a non-profit conservation organisation that takes on the complete responsibility for the rehabilitation and long-term management of national parks and protected areas in partnership with governments and local communities. With the largest counter-poaching force and the most amount of area under protection for any one NGO in Africa, African Parks manages 11 national parks and protected areas covering six and a half million hectares in eight countries: Benin, Central African Republic, Chad, the Democratic Republic of Congo, the Republic of Congo, Malawi, Rwanda and Zambia. Visit african-parks.org.

About the author: José Pliya is a Director of the National Agency for the Heritage and Tourism of Benin. www.revealingbenin.com

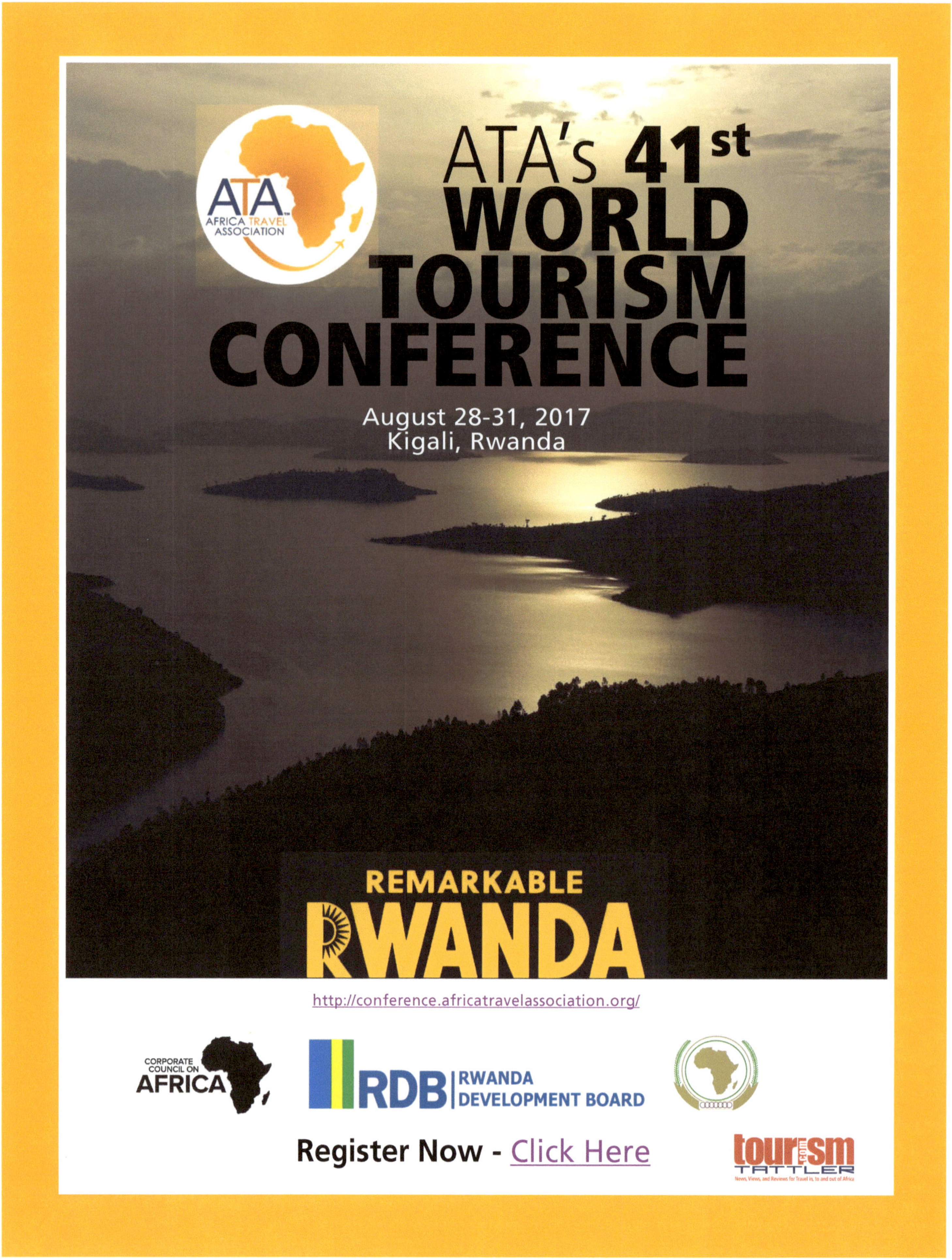

ASSOCIATION EVENT MEDIA PARTNER

ATA's 41st WORLD TOURISM CONFERENCE

August 28-31, 2017
Kigali, Rwanda

REMARKABLE RWANDA

http://conference.africatravelassociation.org/

Register Now - Click Here

DESTINATIONS

Exploring Mauritius Resorts

Mauritius sunset viewed from The Cenizaro Residence.

Mauritius really is an unspoilt Indian Ocean island, highly recommended as a destination for honeymoons, young families or retirement couples. The resorts are excellent, the service wonderful, the rooms thoroughly thought through, and the food is local, fresh and delicious.

By Adam Jacot de Boinod

DESTINATIONS

Idyllic coral sand beach at Four Seasons Resort.

Four Seasons Resort

My first resting spot, the glamorous Four Seasons Resort, lies on the east coast at Anahita. It opened in 2008 and is comprised of different grades of villa – all thoroughly thought through. It's classy. It's all bridges, bicycles and buggies along fresh concrete alleyways. Perfect for kids as well as perfunctory for the demands on the staff. It attracts chiefly a British clientele though Dutch, French, Chinese and Koreans make up most of the rest.

The hotel's own golf course, it's original *raison d'être*, was designed by Ernie Els while the one opposite on the Île aux Cerfs was by Bernhard Langer. The hourly option of a boat shuttle to the Île aux Cerfs is highly recommended. Here I stepped off the quay into a secluded cove only minutes away. A truly idyllic paradise.

The whole stretch of beach to myself. Bliss!

More Info: www.fourseasons.com/mauritius

Lux Le Morne

At my next hotel, Lux Le Morne, the rooms have a neutral décor. Lots of decking, wood and white with no need mercifully for any embellishment. The foyer is cool and clean.

Outside my rooms the gardeners play 'hook and catch' with coconuts using an averruncator (a long stick with shears for cutting high branches). Next to them there's even a "Tree of Wishes" on which guests tag notes containing their personal dreams.

And for parents there is the relief of islands in the middle of creatively shaped swimming pools from which to watch over their kids' safety from all angles. Perfect for a young family.

More Info: www.luxresorts.com/en/hotel-mauritius/luxlemorne

Hole number 10 at the Four Seasons signature golf course.

The creatively shaped swimming pool at Lux Le Morne.

About the author: Adam Jacot de Boinod worked for Stephen Fry on the first series of QI, the BBC programme. While researching this article, Adam had support from Priority Pass, Gatwick Express, and the Holiday Place (www.holidayplace.co.uk).

The Colonial Ocean Front-Suite at The Residence.

The Cenizaro Residence

The rooms at The Residence have beautiful white shutters and outside there are gazebos for quiet contemplation. The few lights on the trees at night make the leaves flow like an orchestra as the palm trees flutter. A perfect environment for dining in the choice of two restaurants: The Plantation, the lovely airy outdoor hall of an original planter's house by the beach which has a menu befitting a gourmet. And The Verandah which offers the right variety as a high-class buffet for those who typically stay more than a week.

All felt invigorating and new, even though The Residence Mauritius has been open for eighteen years. It's the English who are the main punters who typical stay for two weeks. And now increasingly come the Chinese, typically for only five days and only ever the once. I wish I had had two weeks here.

More Info: www.cenizaro.com/theresidence/mauritius

The Hideaways – Stargazer

So on to my final place to stay – membership of The Hideaways Club Classic Collection portfolio gives one access to properties all over the world. It's perfect for someone who doesn't want to be restricted to one location or have the hazzle of maintenance. As tennis player Tim Henman says, *"With the Hideaways Club I have a wide variety of beautiful properties in stunning locations that I can use year round, plus the potential growth of my investment."*

The master bedroom is the only upstairs room and being the only distinguishing feature from the other Mauritian Hideaways property called Hibiscus. Stargazer was built in 2011 as part of Heritage Villas it gave me free access to the Golf Course, Hotels Awani and Telfair and to the C Beach Club (C for Coast and the "Place to C, the place to B" being the chant)! All very spoiling on a very unspoilt island!

More Info: www.thehideawaysclub.com

The Plantation Restaurant at The Residence overlooking the sea.   *The Hideaways Club Hiniscus at Bel Ombre Maurtitius.*

DESTINATIONS

Quick Guide to Southern Africa

The Regional Tourism Organisation of Southern Africa (RETOSA) is a Southern African Development Community (SADC) body responsible for the development of tourism and regional destination marketing across 15 Southern Africa countries: Angola, Botswana, the Democratic Republic of Congo, Lesotho, Madagascar, Malawi, Mauritius, Mozambique, Namibia, Seychelles, South Africa, Swaziland, Tanzania, Zambia and Zimbabwe. RETOSA aims to increase tourism to the region through sustainable development and initiatives, effective destination marketing, and improved regional competitiveness.

To achieve this, RETOSA works in close cooperation with the member states' ministries of tourism, national tourism organisations, the private sector, media partners and international cooperating partners.

These 15 countries offer unique opportunities for business or leisure trips. You will be enchanted by the region's warm people, its beauty and natural wonders, and its unmistakable pulse – sometimes slow, sometimes thrilling, and always invigorating!

info@retosa.co.za | +27 (0)11 315 2420/1 | +27 (0)11 315 9752/3 | www.retosa.co.za

COUNTRY	ANGOLA	BOTSWANA
	Situated right on the Atlantic Ocean, Angola is a budding tourist destination with unspoilt beaches, teeming game reserves and a vibrant culture. Rapidly revitalising itself after the end of the civil war in 2002, the country has one of the fastest growing economies in the world, offering adventurous exploration and lucrative tourism investment opportunities.	A peaceful and prosperous country, Botswana is hailed as one of Africa's most stable democracies - an achievement reflected in the contented, friendly atmosphere which greets tourists in this, the homeland of the Batswana. A top tourist attraction is the Kalahari Desert, covering 70 per cent of the country, while the Okavango River delta in the north boasts abundant and richly diverse wildlife.
CAPITAL	**Luanda**	**Gaborone**
PLACES TO SEE	Luanda and Luanda's beaches: Ilha do Cabo, Mussulo, Palmeirinhas, Corimba and Santiago. Lubango and the Leba Pass, Kissama National Park, Iona National Park	Okavango Delta, Makgadikgadi Pans and Nxai Pans National Park, Chobe National Park, Central Kalahari Game Reserve
MAJOR ACTIVITIES	Beaches and water sports in Luanda; game viewing, bird watching and river cruises in the Kissama National Park; climbing the Tunda-Vala volcanic fissure; driving the Leba Pass; photographing the dunes in the Iona National Park.	Water safaris, walking and elephant-back safaris, and game-viewing by aircraft/helicopter in the Okavango Delta; 4x4 wilderness travelling in the Central Kalahari Game Reserve.
AIRPORT / S	Luanda	Sir Seretse Khama International Airport in Gaborone, but the Maun and Kasane Airports up north are more popular among tourists.
MAIN LANGUAGES	Portuguese, several local dialects	English, Setswana
CURRENCY	Kwanza (AOA)	Pula (BWP)
TIME ZONE	GMT +1	GMT +2
CLIMATE	Tropical in the north, drier plateau in the centre and arid in the south. Average coastal summer temperature 21 °C, 16 °C in winter.	Semi-arid, hot and dry with summer rainfall. Summer temperatures can reach 44°C, while in winter the average day temperature is 25°C, although it turns cold at night.
TOURISM INVESTMENT OPPORTUNITES	Hotels, water sports, game reserves, infrastructure	Lodges and activities in the Kgalagadi Transfrontier Park
MORE INFORMATION	E-mail: angola@angola.org www.angola.org/tourism.html	E-mail: board@botswanatourism.co.bw www.botswanatourism.co.bw

Experience the African Dream

Travelling in Southern Africa is an unforgettable experience. It's a world in 15 countries.

Expect vibrantly contrasting colours, scents, tastes, textures and sounds against a backdrop of endlessly varying topography, climate and tradition. A multi-country journey in this enticingly diverse region promises to be the holiday or business trip of a lifetime. Here, you will make the kind of memories that you will carry with you always – memories that will bring you back again and again.

There are 18 Transfrontier Conservation Areas (TFCAs) that cut across the major eco-regions of SADC member states. These are cross-border conservation areas aimed at preserving wildlife corridors and promoting sustainable management of natural resources and biodiversity. TFCAs represent some of the most important ecosystems in the region, covering an area of around 500 000km².

Experience the African Dream - *Diversity, Humanity, Climate and Wilderness.*

DEMOCRATIC REPUBLIC OF THE CONGO (DRC)	LESOTHO	MADAGASCAR
One of the largest countries in Africa, the DR Congo boasts the second largest rain forest in the world and is home to Africa's most powerful river, the Congo River, and five World Heritage Sites. It is also known for its rare animal species, including the chimpanzee, the bonobo, the mountain gorilla, the okapi and the white rhino.	Lush and breathtakingly beautiful, Lesotho is aptly known as The Mountain Kingdom. It boasts some of the highest and most scenic mountain peaks in Southern Africa, as well as a collection of top-class resorts and lodges and even snow!	East of Africa, in the Indian Ocean lies this idyllic piece of earth, split off from the African mainland millions of years ago. As an island - uninhabited until seafarers from Southeast Asia and Africa arrived 1500 to 2 000 years ago Madagascar's isolation has preserved unique species such as the endangered lemur and ancient baobab trees.
Kinshasa Kinshasa, Congo River by boat, Lake Tanganyika and Lake Kivu, Kahuzi-Biega National Park	**Maseru** Maseru, Thaba Bosiu, Sehlabathebe National Park, Katse Dam in the Malibamatso Valley, Thabana Ntlenyana Tourism	**Antananarivo** Antananarivo, Avenue du Baobab at Morondava, Reserve speciale de L'a narana, Snorkeling at Ifaty, Mangily and Madio Rano
Cruising on the Congo River; sight-seeing in Kinshasha; visiting Lake Kivu and the volcanoes of the Virunga mountain range; boating, rafting or hiking through the rainforest; visiting the mountain gorillas.	Climbing Thaba Bosiu; shopping in Maseru; game viewing, bird watching and pony trekking in the Sehlabathebe National Park; enjoying water sports at the Katse Dam; skiing in the Maloti Mountains.	Snorkelling and diving at Ifaty; visiting the lemurs and the Ankarana Reserve; sight-seeing in Antananarivo
N'djili, Kisangani, Lubumbashi	Moshoeshoe International Airport - Maseru	Ivato International Airport
French, Lingala, Kikongo, Swahili, Tshiluba	English, Sesotho	French, Malagasy, English
Franc (CDF)	Loti (LSL)	Aviary (MGA)
GMT +1 to +2	GMT + 2	GMT +3
Tropical, hot and humid. Day temperatures reach around 30°C.	The rainy season stretches from October to April, with summer maximum temperatures of 32°C and higher. In winter, minimums drop below freezing and snow is common.	Rainy season November to April with average summer temperature of 20°C, which drops to just below 15°C in winter.
World Heritage Sites	Resorts, accommodation in the Maloti Drakensberg Transfrontier Conservation Area.	World Heritage Sites
E-mail: ont_rdcongo@yahoo.fr www.freewebs.com/drcongotourisme/english.htm	E-mail: ltdc@ltdc.org.ls www.ltdc.org.ls	E-mail: ontm@moov.mg / direction@ontm.mg www.madagascar-tourism.com

DESTINATIONS

COUNTRY	MALAWI	MAURITIUS
	Called the warm heart of Africa, Malawi is a paradise of abundant wildlife, waterfalls and lakes. Most famous for the crystal-clear Lake Malawi and the rugged terrain of the Great Rift Valley, the country offers unforgettable travelling extremes.	Described as a sparkling crystal in the turquoise waters of the Indian Ocean, Mauritius is best known for its stunning beaches, luxury resorts and water sports. World-class golf courses, fascinating history and warm, welcoming people all add to the appeal.
CAPITAL	**Lilongwe**	**Port Louis**
PLACES TO SEE	Blantyre is the commercial and industrial centre Lake Malawi National Park, Chongoni Rock Art Area, Mulanje Mountain, Liwonde Nyika and Kasungu National Parks, Lengwe, Majete and Nkhotakota Game Reserves	Le Morne Brabant, historical Mauritius Gymkhana Golf Club, Caudan Waterfront in Port Louis, Black River Gorges National Park, beaches
MAJOR ACTIVITIES	Kayaking, snorkelling and scuba-diving off the pristine beaches of Lake Malawi; horse-back safaris in Nyika National Park; exploring the Chongoni rock art; climbing Mount Mulanje.	Snorkelling, scuba diving and 'undersea strolls'; water sports such as kayaking, jet skiing, parasailing and windsurfing; hiking in the Black River Gorges National Park; visiting Le Morne Brabant.
AIRPORT / S	Kamuzu International Airport (Lilongwe), Chileka (Blantyre)	Sir Seewoosagur Ramgoolam International Airport
MAIN LANGUAGES	English, Chichewa	English, French, Mauritian Creole
CURRENCY	Kwacha (MWK)	Rupee (MUR)
TIME ZONE	GMT +2	GMT +4
CLIMATE	Hot in the low-lying south, moderate in the northern highlands. In summer, the day temperatures are 30°C+, and in winter they drop to 16 °C.	Tropical, warm, dry winter May to November, wet and humid summer November to May with a possibility of cyclones.
TOURISM INVESTMENT OPPORTUNITES	Accommodation in Liwonde National Park, Cape Maclear, hotels, and Nyika conservancy	Hospitality property development
MORE INFORMATION	E-mail: *info@visitmalawi.mw* *www.visitmalawi.mw*	E-mail: *vivek@mtpa.mu* *www.tourism-mauritius.mu*

DESTINATIONS

  **MOZAMBIQUE**	  **NAMIBIA** Namibia Tourism Board	  **SEYCHELLES** the seychelles islands another world
Shimmering oceans, azure skies and a history steeped in rich culture and adventure make Mozambique the ideal destination for every type of traveller, from honeymooners to backpackers. The mild temperatures of the Indian Ocean currents and the stunning beaches are also a tempting drawcard to many scuba-divers, spearfishermen and anglers.	Arid and with sparse vegetation, Namibia is a land of breathtaking beauty and splendour. In this second least densely populated country in the world, travellers can explore the deep ravines of the Fish River Canyon, the timeless beauty of the Namib Desert and the vibrant, friendly towns and cities.	The Seychelles can truly be described, without exaggeration, as paradise on earth. This spectacular necklace of 41 granite and 74 coral islands in the Indian Ocean is a land of perpetual summer, and is renowned for some of the best beaches in the world.
Maputo Maputo, Bazaruto Archipelago, Ilha de Mozambique, Gorongosa National Park, Pemba, Wimbi Beach	**Windhoek** Fish River Canyon, Sossusvlei, Namib Desert, Skeleton Coast, Swakopmund, Lüderitz, Etosha National Park, Windhoek	**Victoria** The Aldabra Atoll: A UNESCO World Heritage Site, Cousin Island Special Reserve, The Vallée de Mai: A World Heritage Site
Kayaking, sailing, dhow trips and snorkelling; visiting the Bazaruto Marine Park and the historical Ilha de Mozambique; game viewing and bird watching in the Gorongosa National Park.	Taking a balloon ride over the dunes of Sossusvlei; hiking in the Fish River Canyon; flying over the the Skeleton Coast; taking a safari in the Etosha National Park.	Water sports, Surfing, Wine tasting, Scenery, Safari, sailing, Golf, Honeymoon, Fishing, Arts
Maputo, Pemba	Chief Hosea Kutako International Airport, Windhoek and Walvis Bay	Seychelles International Airport, Pointe la rue
Portuguese, Swahili	English, Afrikaans, German, Oshiwambo	English, French, and Creole
Metical (MZN)	Dollar (NAD) 1 NAD	Rupee (SCR) 1 SCR
GMT +2	GMT +1	GMT +2
Tropical, with rainfall from December to April and a possibility of cyclones. Summer temperatures exceed 30°C, and the rest of the year the average is 25°C.	The driest in Africa. An average summer temperature of 30°C, which drops to 20°C in winter.	Tropical, 28-32°C
Activities and accommodation in the Great Limpopo Transfrontier Park.	The Waterfront Development in Katima Mulilo, Kavango-Zambezi Transfrontier Conservation Area	Marine
E-mail: *info@visitmozambique.ne* www.visitmozambique.net	E-mail: *media@namibiatourism.com.na* www.namibiatourism.com.na	E-mail: *info@stoza.com* www.seychelles.travel

DESTINATIONS

COUNTRY	SOUTH AFRICA	SWAZILAND
	The diversity of its landscape, its game reserves, its lush and scenic coastal cities, its strong economy and excellent transport infrastructure, make South Africa a favourite destination.	Swaziland is one of Africa's smallest countries, but it boasts a rich history and culture. Its game and nature reserves are highly recommended for Big Five game viewing. There are also several golf clubs with excellent courses, such as the Royal Swazi Golf Course.
CAPITAL	**Pretoria** (executive) Cape Town (legislative)	**Mbabane**
PLACES TO SEE	Garden Route, Cape winelands, Kruger National Park and other game reserves, Kgalagadi Transfrontier Park, Drakensberg mountains, Cape Town, Durban and Johannesburg	Ezulwini and Malkerns Valleys, Hlane Royal National Park, Swazi cultural village in Mantenga Nature Reserve, King Sobhuza II Memorial Park, Mlawula and Malolotja Nature Reserves
MAJOR ACTIVITIES	Taking a cable car to the top of Table Mountain; game viewing, safaris and bird watching in the Kruger National Park; meandering along the Garden Route; wine-tasting in the wine region; water sports and golfing at the coastal resorts.	Visiting the Swazi Cultural Village and the King Sobhuza II Memorial Park; horse-back safaris and guided walks in the Hlane Royal National Park; hiking in the The Malolotja Nature Reserve
AIRPORT / S	OR Tambo International Airport, Cape Town, Durban and several smaller airports	Manzini
MAIN LANGUAGES	English, Afrikaans, isiZulu, IsiXhosa, IsiNdebele, Sepedi, Sesotho, Setswana, SiSwati, Tshivenda, Xitsonga	Siswati, English,
CURRENCY	Currency: Rand (ZAR)	LLilangeni (SZL)
TIME ZONE	GMT +2	GMT +2
CLIMATE	Moderate to very hot in the north, with summer temperatures of 40°C and more, to below freezing point at night in winter.	Rainfall from December to April. Summer temperatures reach 40°C in the lowveld, and winter temperatures on the Highveld drop to below 15°C.
TOURISM INVESTMENT OPPORTUNITES	Transfrontier Conservation Areas	Accommodation, Lubombo Transfrontier Conservation Area.
MORE INFORMATION	E-mail: info@southafrica.net www.southafrica.net	E-mail: infodesk@tourismauthority.org.sz www.welcometoswaziland.com

DESTINATIONS

  **TANZANIA** The Land of Kilimanjaro, Zanzibar and The Serengeti	  **ZAMBIA**	  **ZIMBABWE**
Home to Mount Kilimanjaro, the tallest mountain in Africa, and Lake Tanganyika, the world's longest and second deepest fresh water lake, Tanzania is an awe-inspiring country. Other major tourist attractions include the Serengeti National Park, in particular the annual wildebeest migration, and the popular holiday island of Zanzibar.	Epitomising the real Africa, Zambia is home to natural wonders such as the thundering Zambezi River and world-famous Victoria Falls. Nature reserves and transfrontier conservation enable the visitor to view wildlife it its natural habitat. Known for its welcoming people, rich culture and fascinating drumming and dancing rituals, Zambia is the ideal adventure destination.	In addition to abundant wildlife and exceptional game parks, Zimbabwe offers a rich variety for tourists that includes the Great Zimbabwe ruins, the spectacular Victoria Falls and the mighty Zambezi River. Numerous activities – including bungee jumping from the railway bridge and white-water rafting - have evolved around this famous landmark.
Dodoma (Political) and **Dar es Salaam** (Administrative, commercial) Mount Kilimanjaro, Serengeti National Park, Ngorongoro Crater, Zanzibar, Lake Tanganyika and Lake Victoria, Arusha National Park, Dar Es Salaam	**Lusaka** Lusaka, South Luangwa National Park, Lower Zambezi National Park, Lake Kariba, Victoria Falls	**Harare** Harare, Victoria Falls, Lake Kariba, Hwange National Park, Great Zimbabwe National Monument, Khami Ruins National Monument, Matobo Hills near Bulawayo
Climbing Mount Kilimanjaro; visiting Zanzibar; game viewing and bird watching in the Serengeti; visiting the Ngorogoro Crater; taking a boat trip on Lake Victoria.	Scenic flights over the Victoria Falls; swimming in the Devil's Pool above the falls; white-water rafting and other water sports; river cruises; elephant-back rides; walking with lions, game drives in the Mosi-oa-Tunya National Park; walking safaris in the South Luangwa National Park.	Flights over the Victoria Falls; sunset cruises on the Zambezi river; bungee jumping off the Victoria Falls Bridge; river rafting and other water sports; swinging through the gorge; elephant-back rides; walking with lions; visiting the Great Zimbabwe National Monument.
Julius Nyerere International Airport in Dar es Salaam and Kilimanjaro, International Airport in Arusha	Lusaka International Airport, Livingstone	Harare, flights to Victoria Falls
Swahili, English	English, Chinyanja and 72 local dialects	Shona, Ndebele, English
Shilling (TZS)	Kwatcha (ZMK)	Dollar (ZWD)
GMT +3	GMT +2	GMT +2
Tropical Summer temperatures 20°C in the highlands, in winter down to 10°C. Elsewhere 25 31°C in summer and 15 20°C in winter.	Tropical, the rainy season stretching from November to April. Average temperatures of above 20°C over most of the country.	Moderate, wet from November to May. An average summer temperature of 21°C, down to 14°C in winter.
Conference and eco-tourism	Wildlife-based activities, Transfrontier Conservation Area.	Resort development, Wildlife based activities, Tourism frontier conservation areas, Accommodation and Tourism infrastructure
E-mail: *info@tanzaniatourism.go.tz* *www.tanzaniatouristboard.go.tz*	E-mail: z*ntb@zambiatourism.org.zm* *www.zambiatourism.com*	E-mail: *info@ztazim.co.zw* or *marketing@ztazim.co.zw* / *www.zimbabwetourism.net*

LGBT Pride Month 2017

The month of June is unofficially recognised as Lesbian, Gay, Bisexual, and Transgender (LGBT) Pride Month. How does Africa fare in terms of LGBT rights and what is the potential of LGBT Tourism?

By **Des Langkilde**.

LGBT Rights in Africa

With the exception of South Africa, LGBT rights in Africa are very limited in comparison to many other parts of the world. According to Wikipedia, out of the 55 states recognised by the United Nations or the African Union or both, the International Gay and Lesbian Association stated in 2015 that homosexuality is outlawed in 34 African countries. Human Rights Watch notes that another two countries, Benin and the Central African Republic, do not outlaw homosexuality, but have certain laws which apply differently to heterosexual and homosexual individuals.

Homosexual activity between adults has never been criminalised in Burkina Faso, Central African Republic, Republic of the Congo, Ivory Coast, Democratic Republic of the Congo, Djibouti, Equatorial Guinea, Gabon, Madagascar, Mali, Niger, and Rwanda.

In Sudan, southern Somalia and northern Nigeria acts of homosexuality are punishable by death, while in Uganda, Tanzania, and Sierra Leone, offenders can receive life imprisonment for homosexual acts.

In addition to criminalising homosexuality, Nigeria has enacted legislation that makes it illegal for heterosexual family members, allies, and friends of the LGBT to be supportive. According to Nigerian law, a heterosexual ally *'who administers, witnesses, abets or aids'* any form of gender non-conforming and homosexual activity could receive a 10-year jail sentence.

Of the 34 African countries who protect LGBT rights to some extent, South Africa has the most liberal attitude, with a constitution that guarantees gay and lesbian rights and legalises same-sex marriage.

Potential of LGBT Tourism in South Africa

During the 2017 African Travel Indaba, I met up with Jason Fiddler – the founding Chairperson and Key Accounts Manager of the KwaZulu-Natal Gay & Lesbian Tourism Association (KZNGALTA), founded in 2004, which makes it the oldest such association in Africa. I asked Jason for his insights into the potential of LGBT community as a niche tourism sector.

"LGBT tourism is no longer the niche market that it was in the 90's and early 2000s. LGBT, or pink travellers as I like to refer to them, have definitely gone mainstream. In 2012 the first UNWTO report on LGBT Tourism reported on figures of around US$165 billion per annum as the market's global value. In 2016, OutNow, the global research firm on whose data the UNWTO relied, presented at WTM London a revised value of US$211 billion. That's a staggering 27% increase in spending value over 5 years! I don't know any other tourism market showing that kind of growth.

"Globally we're seeing LGBT communities becoming more assertive of their rights, being more open and travelling more, both domestically and internationally. The second UNWTO Report on LGBT Tourism speaks much more in depth about this subject and gives some great case studies. For example, and this is from my observational experience as chief marshal of the Durban LGBTI Pride March, in 2011 when we began, we had around 800 people walking, of which approximately 50 had come down from Gauteng province to attend. In 2016, I head counted around 1500 walking, of which around 500 were from outside Durban and predominantly from Gauteng. They'd specifically come to support an important LGBT gathering and enjoy our great winter weather too - so tourism grew and an LGBT rights event was the catalyst," says Fiddler.

LGBT Market Research in South Africa

In April 2012 Lunch Box Media (LBM) commissioned Qualitative Quarter to conduct a nationwide survey among the South African gay community. In the preface to the LBM Consumer Profile 2012, LBM estimates the size of the LGBT community in South Africa to be around 4.9 million people. The report found that gay people have a higher percentage of disposable income and spend more on luxury items. In terms of travel, the report found that 44% of survey respondents travel more than once a year with 34% taking a holiday at least once a year. 10% indicated travel to international destinations, while 35% travel locally. Of these, 25% travel out of season and 9% in-season.

"We've always seen domestic pink travel as important for our provincial growth, especially as KwaZulu-Natal is closer to the key Gauteng source market than say, the Western Cape is. We're definitely an affordable destination and this plays importantly into travel research out of the USA that says that LGBT travellers are predominantly seeking mid-range product, but staying longer," says Fiddler.

"Key factors to note about domestic pink travellers are that they travel throughout the year (although there's a growing number of LGBT families with children nowadays) and not just seasonally; they tend to spend extra time on a trip by at least 1-2 nights whenever possible; they can be quite spontaneous and respond quickly to time-specific promotions; they have high standards and are aspirational, so, therefore, many will choose an affordable product but expect above-average services, facilities, and amenities – this means that little extra effort on the part of the accommodation provider, for instance, goes a very long way to building the travel loyalty this market is very capable of."

Potential of International LGBT Tourism

In his article 'Pride Month: How is LGBT tourism doing these days?' Juergen T Steinmetz, publisher of eTurboNews sheds some enlightening insights to marketing to LGBT travellers. "LGBT tourism is doing very well right now, but reliable estimates of global spend by LGBT travelers are difficult to come by. Often times you hear that LGBT travelers in the United States spend about $65 billion per year, but this isn't backed up by solid research.

"As someone who's chronicled and, in part, helped shape LGBT travel since 1998, I can see many changes. More and more major brands are targeting the LGBT travel segment than ever before. LGBT travelers have more options. Many years ago, gay travelers would have to choose from a few spots like Mykonos, Provincetown, Key West, Sitges or Palm Springs. These were among the few places where a gay or lesbian person could be with a same-sex partner without worrying that they would attract unfriendly attention, or worse, harassment and violence. Today, gays are far more widely welcomed. Thank goodness, times are changing!"

In terms of LGBT rights, Steinmentz says; "There are over 73 countries where homosexuality is criminalized, and many of those are in the Caribbean, Africa and Asia. Usually in Asian countries they are socially homophobic, meaning that marriage (and raising children) is the most important aspect of their culture. For visitors, they really don't care as long as the visitor (male, female, gay or straight) doesn't flaunt their sexuality. Thailand is very gay-friendly. Taiwan may legalize same-sex marriage. Even China – which is very traditional – has gay bars and a vibrant gay community."

Can LGBT tourism make a country more accepting? "As soon as gays have more rights in a country – most notably marriage equality – marketers are right there targeting the lucrative gay marriage and honeymoon market. We saw this time and time again in Canada and the United States. That said, I believe that being our authentic selves while abroad – especially to countries that aren't as familiar with gay people – is the best way to open minds and build bridges," Steinmentz concludes.

Why LGBT Pride Month is Celebrated in June

In an opinion piece posted on medium.com, Davia Sobelman notes that; "Two historic (USA) milestones for the LGBT community occurred in June: the notorious Stonewall riots of '69 and the iconic legalization of same-sex marriage. Among other critical points in LGBT history, June has become the month to celebrate pride. Whether the community is coming together in heartache or triumph, 30 days are dedicated to discussing how far we have come, and how far we still need to go."

"Awareness months give a community of people an opportunity to receive recognition and speak on their importance. Pride Month does just that – it unifies people to study our history, analyze the present, and plan for the future. In doing so, we get a glimpse as to what one community has suffered, conquered, and still faces.

"With Pride Month here, we encourage all those participating in the festivities to be aware of the hardships this community has endured – as they are still fighting for inclusivity and acceptance. Becoming familiar with LGTB history is crucial in identifying why there is a reason to celebrate in the first place. Although the fight for same-sex marriage is now a reality, the inequality lives on," concludes Sobelman.

Key LGBT Pride Events

South Africa:
- Durban Pride 24 June 2017
- Pretoria Pride 07 October 2017
- Johannesburg Pride 28 October 2017
- Cape Town Pride end March 2018
- Pink Loerie Mardi Gras & Arts Festival Knysna 27 April - 1 May 2018.

International:
- Gandia Pride 05 June 2017
- ARN Culture Pride 05 June 2017
- LGBT Tourism Forum of Brazil 13 June 2017.

Key LGBT Associations

South Africa:
- KwaZulu-Natal Gay & Lesbian Tourism Association: www.kzngalta.org.za
- Durban Pride: www.durbanpride.org.za

International:
- International Gay & Lesbian Travel Association: www.iglta.org

www.ingramcontent.com/pod-product-compliance
Lightning Source LLC
Chambersburg PA
CBHW041306180526
45172CB00003B/989